What Will Help Me?

BOOKS BY JAMES E. MILLER

What Will Help Me? / How Can I Help?
When You're Ill or Incapacitated / When You're the Caregiver
How Will I Get Through the Holidays?
One You Love Is Dying
When You Know You're Dying
Winter Grief, Summer Grace
Autumn Wisdom
The Caregiver's Book
Welcoming Change
A Pilgrimage Through Grief
Helping the Bereaved Celebrate the Holidays
A Little Book for Preachers
Effective Support Groups
The Practical Art of Journal Writing
One You Love Has Died
When a Man Faces Grief / A Man You Know Is Grieving
Finding Hope
When Mourning Dawns

VIDEOTAPES BY JAMES E. MILLER

Invincible Summer
Listen to Your Sadness
How Do I Go On?
Nothing Is Permanent Except Change
By the Waters of Babylon
We Will Remember
Gaining a Heart of Wisdom
Awaken to Hope
Be at Peace
The Natural Way of Prayer
You Shall Not Be Overcome
The Grit and Grace of Being a Caregiver
Why Yellow?
Common Bushes Afire

What Will Help Me?

12 Things to Remember
When You Have Suffered A Loss

James E. Miller

WILLOWGREEN®
PUBLISHING

To Ken,
whose spirit teaches me so much.

I am indebted to Clare Barton, Lee Battey, Sue Devito,
John Gantt, Dick Gilbert, Paul Johnson, Gail Kittleson, Patty Lee,
Jennifer Levine, Bernie Miller, John Peterson, and John Schneider
for their thoughtful editorial suggestions.

Sources cited include Helen Hayes, *My Life in Three Acts*,
San Diego, 1989; Katherine Mansfield, *Journal of Katherine
Mansfield*, New York, 1927; Rainer Maria Rilke, *Letters to a
Young Poet*, New York, 1984, and Colin Murray Parkes,
Bereavement, New York, 1972.

Willowgreen Publishing
10351 Dawson's Creek Boulevard, Suite B
Fort Wayne, Indiana 46825
260/490-2222

jmiller@willowgreen.com

Library of Congress Catalog
Card Number: 00-92433

ISBN 1-885933-19-3

Someone you love has died. Perhaps you expected this death and tried to prepare yourself for it. Maybe instead your loss came suddenly and with complete surprise. However it happened, your life has changed—it is not the same. You are not the same either.

You may be in a time when each day is an agony for you. You may feel you cannot escape your anguish, no matter what you do. You may know what it's like to wish to fall asleep so you can be rid of the pain for awhile, only to discover that your pain follows you into your dreams. Then when you awaken, it stabs at you once again, sometimes with a freshness that takes your breath away. You may wonder how long you must go on living like this. You may question if your life will ever get better, if there will be anything to hope for again, or anything to live for. Some days you may feel like giving up.

On the other hand, it's possible that this death is not the worst thing that's ever happened to you. You may be able to recall other times in your life that were more trying, more troubling. You may still find, however, that this experience you're going through leaves you shaken and unnerved. Your feelings may rush over you unpredictably. You may surprise yourself with how much you hurt.

However long this time of grief lasts, chances are it will seem too long. Almost always it goes on longer than people around you expect, especially those who do not understand how much your life has been affected. They may be anxious for you to "return to normal." They may coax you to do that more quickly than you're ready. They may not be prepared for the fact that your "old normal" may not be your "new normal."

Indeed, your grieving may go on longer than you want it to as well. You may tire of always feeling tired. You may grow weary of your weariness. You may feel weakened by the continuing pain and discomfort. Your task, though, is to remain in your pain long enough—not an hour longer than you need to, but not an hour less than your loss demands either. However uncomfortable this time is for you—and without doubt, some days can be very distressing—still, your grief is serving a purpose. It is helping you heal. In fact, it is only by grieving that you will heal.

The words that follow were written for people like you as you grieve the death of someone who has been an important part of your life. The purpose of these words is to lead you through these days with as much comfort, security, and hope as is reasonably possible. But this book cannot take away your hurt. In fact, it dare not take away your hurt. Perhaps what you read here will ease your pain a bit. Perhaps you will be able to see a ray of light ahead. But it is only by going through your pain that you will come to accept what has happened and eventually arrive at another place in your life that lies on the far side of your grief.

If you remember nothing else, remember this: you are not alone. Others have previously made the journey that you are making now, and they have returned to lead lives that are full and rich and engaging. Others are making a journey like yours right now and they are learning at the same time you're learning. There are others around you who wish to support you and do what they can for you. Companions wait for you along the way. You may not have experienced that yet, but they're there.

Not all the thoughts written here will apply equally to your situation. Some will fit better than others. Take the ideas and suggestions that suit you best and offer you the most. Then leave the rest for other people, or for another time in your life.

May you find here a sense of assurance that all is not lost and a sense of hope that you will eventually feel better. Yes, this experience hurts. Yes, the way before you may seem long. Yes, what is yours to do may be difficult for you to do. But no, you do not have to be completely overcome. No, you do not have to travel entirely alone. No, you do not have to go through this experience blindly.

You can do what you may fear you cannot. You can find ways to help yourself and ways to be helped. You can in time use this as a time of growth. You can gradually return to life again. In other words, you can heal. You can be whole again. You can be fully you. You can, and by going all the way through the grieving process, you will. I believe that.

Jim Miller

1
The best way to handle your feelings
is not to "handle" them but to feel them.

People may be giving you less-than-helpful messages about dealing with this death you have experienced. Here is a sampling:

• "You're handling your loss very well." What many people mean by this feedback is that you're not crying too much or acting too upset—you seem fairly normal. Maybe you're being stoic. Whatever others say, that's not necessarily the best way to grieve.

• "You must be strong now." Often you're expected to be strong for other people, usually those in your own family. Sometimes you're told to be strong just for yourself, so you can deal with all you're facing. Another translation may lie beneath these words: "Don't look like you feel weak or unsure."

• "Cheer up. You'll be over this soon." Another translation for "cheer up" is "cheer us." Some people don't know what to do when others are sad. They feel uncomfortable around them. They feel doubly uncomfortable when someone stays sad for a long time, which can easily happen during grief, as you well know. People may try to hurry you along with their feedback and their advice, as if to say "Let's get this over with as quickly as we can." They have themselves in mind more than you.

If you're given these sorts of messages, do yourself a favor: pay no attention to them. The best way for you to grieve is by being in touch with whatever emotions come your way. Your feelings may be many or few. They may be gentle or strong or anything in between. They're likely to be unpredictable. But they're not at all a sign that something is wrong with you. Indeed, your feelings are a sign that something is right with you. Someone you love has died and left you, and naturally that hurts. Your life has changed in ways you wish it hadn't. So you grieve. That's the way you eventually begin to feel more like yourself again, and more whole, however long that takes.

You may feel sad, sadder than you thought possible. You may feel depressed, even despairing. You may feel afraid, even without understanding why. You may feel very lonely, even when you're around other people, and sometimes especially when you're around others. You may feel unusually tired, easily distracted, uncharacteristically anxious. You may get angry more easily—angry at others, at yourself, at God, maybe even at the one who died. Some people feel guilty, either for what they've said or done, or for what they've not said or not done.

Another sensation you may have is this: almost no feeling at all. You may feel empty and numb. That's a common reaction, especially at first. It's a sign that your body and mind may be protecting you until you're more ready to process what has happened.

It takes courage to face all that you must face. It takes a huge amount of energy, and at a time when your reserves are lower than normal. It takes strength and determination to keep doing what is yours to do these days—to feel whatever it is you happen to feel. You have a simple choice. You can experience your feelings in your own way as they come to you, or you can put them off until another time. But you do not have the choice of putting them off forever. Somewhere, somehow, sometime, your feelings will demand your attention. By then they may have grown even stronger and gone even deeper.

Remember: the best way out is always through. The best way beyond your feelings is not by going around them but by going with them.

2
By giving your loss expression, you'll begin to heal.

It's one thing to feel what you feel. It's another to let your feelings take a certain form, a certain expression. Others may be around you when this happens, or maybe you'll be alone. It may be obvious when you're doing this, or maybe it won't. But the more clearly you can express yourself in your own unique ways, the more surely and completely you can heal.

You'll figure out what's right for you as you go along. Some people find that talking with just one other person works best. This might be a friend, a family member, a colleague, or a professional of some sort. Others have enough to say, and enough need to say it, that it seems right to communicate one-on-one with several people. Perhaps you'll want to talk with a person you've long known, but you might also choose someone you've only recently met. You might chat informally at a restaurant or at home, as you take a drive or a walk, by going shopping or fishing. You might be more intentional about your talking by meeting at a certain place for a series of conversations, focusing on what you feel you need to talk about. Another option is to search out a support group made up of people who are going through what you are.

It's important to feel you can trust the person or people to whom you're turning. What you share should be kept in confidence. So find someone who is a good listener, someone who can give you the quiet and the freedom to say what you have to say.

Some people are more comfortable writing about what's going on inside them. Taking the time to construct your thoughts on paper or perhaps on a computer encourages you to be deliberate in a way that talking alone may not provide. If you haven't been a journal writer before, might you become one now? Write as often as you want, but try to write regularly and always write honestly. Your writings can give you a helpful perspective when you read back through them weeks or months later.

You might write long letters to someone you know who wants to hear from you. Or you might compose letters you'll never send—like letters to the one who has died, or to yourself, or to God. You might try your hand at poetry, or in writing a fictional story that's only too true, or maybe the real story of what actually happened in your life.

Sometimes words may not be the right vehicle for your feelings. Who can improve upon tears as a way of expressing one's grief? Did you know that the chemical makeup of your tears of sorrow is quite different from your tears of happiness or relief? Evidence suggests that crying can be healthy for you physically as well as emotionally.

Other wordless means of expression might include working with paint brushes or drawing pencils, with modeling clay or photographic film, with wood or with metal. Some people prefer singing, or playing an instrument, or listening to music that moves or inspires them.

However you choose to express yourself, know that you are encouraging your own healing in doing what you do. You are finding your own way to make sense of what has happened. You are coming to accept, bit by bit, the reality of what all this means. So express yourself in the ways that are natural for you. Do it as often as you want and do it the best way: with feeling.

3
Seldom is this loss only "this loss" for you.

Your internal responses may be caused solely by what has happened to you as a result of this recent death. Indeed, a lot has happened and it can affect you in many different ways. But a single death is more than a single loss. The death of someone close causes other losses too.

The death of a spouse or partner, for example, ripples out in many directions. Depending on the situation, one might lose that other parent for one's children, or the other income-producer for one's family, or that co-worker who did so many things around the house. One might have to change homes, or jobs, or even friends. The death of a child can lead to the loss of dreams, the loss of one's role as parent, the loss of innocence or security. The death of a parent or sibling can involve the loss of part of one's past, among other things. Each of these so-called "secondary losses" needs to be grieved as well.

In addition, the death you're dealing with may bring forth memories of other losses you've experienced. These events may at first seem unrelated to what's happened, but probably they are related. It's common for other deaths you've known to visit you again, including "deaths" like divorces, job losses, disabilities, and various traumatic life events.

One type of loss in particular is likely to reappear—any previous loss you have not yet completely grieved. Perhaps someone close to you died and you did not have the permission or the time or the maturity to adequately mourn their death. This may go back many years in your life. For one reason or another, you may have hidden what you felt, or you may have downplayed what happened, or you may have avoided what you needed to do as a part of your grieving. Maybe you just didn't know any better at the time. Now, much later, your loss presents itself to you again, as if to say, "I haven't gone away yet; there are some things we need to talk through." If you sense that's the case, you might find value in giving yourself the opportunity to look at those previous losses too. You might want to seek out someone who is experienced at understanding what you're going through—a grief counselor, a psychotherapist, or a clergyperson who has training in this area.

And it's not just unresolved losses that float into consciousness again. So do those losses you've already worked through and come to accept. But there's a difference. You feel the original emotions of these types of losses much less keenly. You're more likely to think, "I am at peace with what happened back then." When a former loss reenters your awareness, it may simply be an invitation to look at its meaning at a deeper level than before and in light of the unfolding events in your life.

A reliable wisdom is at work inside you, ready to make this period of your life a time for healing. Trust what is happening. Grieve in the ways that feel right for you. And if people around you don't understand your need to grieve all your various losses, remember that this is your grief, not theirs. Claim it as your own.

4
There is one person who can take care of you better than anyone, and that's you.

Some part of you may want to rely upon another person or other people for care and support. You deserve that, and with good fortune you'll know that experience. But however much others can do for you, there is still much they cannot do. There are some things only you can do.

No one knows what's going on inside you the way you do. No one understands your wants and needs quite like yourself. And certain of those needs and wants cannot be met by another, no matter how much they want to help, no matter how skilled they are—they can only be met by you.

It's important that you get regular exercise, now more than ever. You'll feel better physically, mentally, and emotionally when you do. Obviously no one else can walk for you, or run, or swim. No one else can do calisthenics in your place.

You must oversee your own rest. This might involve going to bed early enough, or napping often enough, or just sitting and relaxing regularly enough. Another person cannot get your rest for you.

The same goes for your eating and drinking. A healthy diet is extremely important, especially now. You need to drink plenty of water and monitor carefully the consumption of any alcohol and other behavior-modifying drugs.

Only you can determine how you'll spend your time. Will you bury yourself in your work or in a flurry of activities as a way of escaping your grief? Or will you find ways to let the reality of this loss into your life, a little at a time? Will you give yourself respites from the stress you experience? And make no mistake: the death of someone close can be one of the most stress-producing events you'll ever know. Will you be lenient about what you expect of yourself during this demanding time?

There are many things you can do to take care of yourself. Here are a few:

• Spend time in nature. Creation has a wonderful way of restoring you and a wise way of reminding you and assuring you.

• Give yourself small gifts from time to time. Depending upon what brings you pleasure, buy yourself a new book, a tape or CD, or an inexpensive piece of artwork. Indulge yourself with something to wear, an evening out, a favorite taste treat. Splurge on a bouquet of fresh flowers. It isn't the cost that counts—it's the thought.

• Choose to be among people you enjoy. Spend time with those who lift you. Stay away from those who sap your energy.

• Find things you like to do with your hands. This often helps calm your mind and heart too, and it can give you a quiet sense of accomplishment.

• Follow up with any desires to learn something new or to try something different. That's a sign that rebirth can be working its way into your life when the time is right.

• Do little things for other people, things you enjoy doing or find meaning in doing. You'll feel better for making a difference in someone's life. You can grieve and still help others at the same time.

Assert your authority to do what no other person in the world can do: to determine what is right for you, and then do something about it. Of course, "doing something about it" may mean giving yourself the freedom to relax and do nothing at all.

5
In allowing others to help you, you help everyone: them and you.

If you are like most people in our culture, this motto has been drummed in: "Be independent. Stand on your own two feet." Then you come to a period in your life like the one you're going through and you realize that your own two feet are somehow not quite enough. You may find yourself wondering, "How independent should I be, and how dependent? How do I know?"

Remember first of all that letting others do things for you during this time is not a sign of weakness or incompetence on your part. Allowing yourself to depend on others for awhile is a sound way of getting through what can be a terribly difficult time. Often it makes sense to lean on others more at the beginning of your grief and then gradually decrease your leaning as time goes along. But that is not always the pattern, nor should it be.

When people offer to help, and when their help is something you want and could use, say "yes." Let them show their concern and share their energy. Permit them to serve as a stabilizing influence during this time which can be known for its instability. Let a sense of community form around you.

This may be a new role for you, one that will take some getting used to. But it's worth it. Why? Because you are worth it. You are worth having other people care about your needs. You are worth the attention they give you and any nurturing they provide you. They're giving you a message: you are valuable to them. In accepting the offers of help that feel right, you send them a similar message: they mean much to you too.

Keep in mind that the people who volunteer to help may need to do that for themselves as well as for you. If they're grieving the same death you're grieving, this can be an important way for them to respond to their own sense of loss. If what saddens them is simply your sadness, then one way they can cope with their feelings is to assist you in those ways that work best for them and for you. Inevitably, those around you will feel a certain helplessness, for there is much they cannot do, as you well know.

Be thankful for those people who make sincere and sensitive offers of help. Accept as many of those offers as feels right for you. Be gracious in any refusals and let people know that you'll entertain other offers in the future. If people say to you, "Let me know if there's anything I can do to help," and you want their help, take them at their word. Let them know. Perhaps you can give them a couple of options and let them choose. Ask people to do those things they feel most competent doing. Always remember that you're in this together—you're both helping and you're both being helped at the same time.

It's possible you may feel there is no one to help you. If you are isolated and alone, you must take the first step. Many communities have a clearinghouse for support services you can call. Find out what programs are available for people in your situation. Try one and see if it helps. It may take a couple of attempts before you know. Another option is to think of a person you'd be comfortable talking with. Contact them and explain that you feel the need to converse, and why. Chances are they'll agree once they understand how important this is to you.

In what seems an unfortunate time, you can know the blessing of having people care for you in ways that can make a real difference as you grieve. And that's fortunate.

6
God may not be finished yet with those who try to give you care.

A popular T-shirt that made the rounds a few years ago had these words printed on it: "Be patient with me. God isn't finished with me yet." You may find it helpful to visualize that T-shirt on some of the people who volunteer to help you, and some of those who don't.

Let's first admit this: those who try to assist you have a difficult role. Some people have had little or no experience with loss and suffering in their own lives. Therefore they may not know what really helps. The whole subject of death and grief is one our modern society generally wants to ignore or cover up. Sadly, in our culture, unlike many other cultures around the world, there are almost no rules that prescribe what others are to do when someone like you is going through grief.

Consequently it should not surprise you if others fall short in the kind of care they give you, or they don't give you. They may avoid talking about your loss, thinking that's what you want, not realizing you may want the opposite. They may avoid broaching the whole subject of death and grief out of their own discomfort, not realizing that almost everyone feels as uncomfortable as they do.

People around you may not give you the opportunity to talk about your loss as much as you desire. They may not be prepared for you to express all the emotion that may want to come out. They may tell you about their own very different and more limited losses, thinking that in making this comparison, they'll forge a bond with you. As you know, this may in reality create more of a distance. People may offer you a variety of cliches, thinking it will help you. Perhaps you've heard some of them already, like, "I know exactly how you feel," or "God doesn't give you more than you can handle," or "Cheer up—it could be worse." Comments like these fail to validate the depth of your feelings and the gravity of what has happened.

Some people may not let you have the privacy you sometimes long for. Others may not give you the follow-up they promise. Some may offer you too much advice and not enough understanding, while others may want to take too much control and leave you too little freedom.

In short, your helpers may be awkward in their helping, just as you sometimes feel awkward in needing their help. How you respond to this delicate situation will be up to you. On the one hand, you may feel tired and out of sorts. Your patience may be wearing thin. You may think you deserve better treatment, and you're prepared to say so. On the other hand, you may not want to make waves. You may hesitate to risk offending anyone who has been important to you. You may be unsure what is right to do.

Probably there will be times when your forgiveness is what will work best. Usually people's hearts are really in the right place, even if that doesn't appear to be the case initially. There may be other times, however, when your heartfelt honesty will be the most helpful. Then you can feel good about being true to yourself and your feelings, hoping that your truthfulness will help others improve their caregiving skills in the future. Sometimes you may choose to speak your thoughts with the full force of your firmness and conviction. Only you can decide.

An old expression goes, "Any adversity not learned from is an adversity wasted." One lesson that may come from this adversity of yours is what good caregiving is all about. That's something you can both learn and teach.

7
Sometimes it makes perfect sense to act a little crazy.

Actress Helen Hayes describes her experience of adjusting to her husband's death in this way: "I was just as crazy as you can be and still be at large. I didn't have any normal moments during those two years. It wasn't just grief, it was total confusion. I was nutty."

Yes, these can be nutty times. You may surprise yourself with how flighty your mind is, how changeable your feelings are. You may do things that don't make sense to you afterward, or even as you're doing them. You may find it difficult to make decisions. Or you may make decisions quite quickly, only to change your mind just as fast and just as often. You may feel like you've lost your center or like you're frazzling at the edges. Close friends may tell you that you're acting a little strange. They may tell you that with their words, but more likely you'll see it in their eyes. You may see it in your own eyes when you look in the mirror.

German dramatist Gotthold Lessing once wrote, "There are things that must cause you to lose your reason or you have none to lose." If this death has really shaken you, and if your pain has been intense, you have plenty of cause to lose your reason for awhile. You may feel and act not quite normal. That happens quite naturally when everything around you feels abnormal.

If there are signs this is happening with you, here are some suggestions:

• First of all, don't panic. You're actually in good company. Lots of people experience "the crazies" as they grieve. Remember that sometimes you need to fall apart a little before you can come back together in a healthier way. Remember also that if you act too usual in a time that's very unusual—well, that's unusual!

• Select a person whom you trust for their forthrightness and maturity, and ask them to be your gauge. If you want feedback about how you're responding, or if you want assistance with your decision-making, turn to this person. Don't attempt to follow the advice of many different people—it won't work.

• Talk things out. Speak what is on your mind and in your heart, including those thoughts that seem irrational. Sometimes it's only after you've spoken such ideas out loud that you can see them for what they really are—a little weird.

• Keep a journal about what's going on inside you. Then go back in a few weeks or months and see how your thinking is changing. Notice the ways you're growing. Then write about that too. Some of the unusualness you feel will begin to drop away.

• Take yourself lightly at times. While your life may feel heavy these days—and justifiably so—it's still possible you may begin to see some humor in what you've said and done. If that's so, smile at yourself. Be understanding and forgiving. Remember some of the goofy things you did so you can one day retell those stories as a way of reassuring someone else, just as Helen Hayes has done for you.

8
Your grieving, timing, and progress in healing are all uniquely yours, and that's as it should be.

Ideas abound in folklore and in books about how you will experience your loss. Some who call themselves professionals have carefully described exactly what you will feel, when you will feel it, and for how long. They have outlined in detail their theories about the clearly-defined stages of grief you will pass through.

Closer to home, you will probably find plenty of people around you who are ready to offer their predictions and prescriptions for what you're going through. Some may lead you to believe that your present experience ought to mimic the one they've had. There will be those who will tell you that you need not grieve certain kinds of deaths very much. The grief over a miscarriage or a stillbirth, for instance, may be minimized by those who don't understand the depth and meaning of such a loss. The death of a parent may be dismissed far too casually with "their time had finally come." The death of a friend may be downplayed because "you weren't related to them."

You may be told one shouldn't mourn another's death too long, no matter how close you've been. You may be advised that the proper length of time for grief is, say, three months, or six months, or a year. You may be informed you'll grieve less if someone's death has been anticipated or you'll grieve more if you've been terribly close to one another.

Pay little attention to those people who give you precise formulas for how you'll go through this time. You are a unique individual, with your own feelings, your own experience of death, your own history of previous losses, your own family influences, your own natural ways of expressing yourself, and many other variables which are no one else's but yours. Learn to trust your own timing. Have faith in your own natural fluctuations. Believe in the guiding wisdom of your own grief.

If your loss is comparatively minor, it may not take you very long to recover. But what is a short time for you may not be a short time for someone else. The difference between a minor and major loss depends on your personal perspective. No one can truly appreciate what this death means for you unless they have lived your life, unless they have had your relationship with the one who died, unless they are going through exactly what you are going through today.

Your grief may last longer than you expect, longer than others are ready for. Sometimes grief can hold on for two years, three years, or even longer. In some cases a person may feel quick, isolated, gradually diminishing pangs of grief over the course of many years, even a lifetime.

Studies confirm that those who have adequate personal support tend to go through times like this with fewer complications. But that's not always the case. Those who must deal with a series of losses, one after another, or with several losses all at the same time, may take longer with their grief. Or they may not. Women and men may respond differently. Or perhaps they won't. You can't always be sure.

No one is going through exactly what you are, no matter who they are. They can't. They don't have your same feelings and personality, your same past and present. So make your way through this experience in the full awareness that this is yours and no one else's. Hold on to your right to be you.

9
Healthy grieving is about more than letting go. It's about keeping a connection too.

"You have to say goodbye to the one who died before you can really move on with your life." Has anyone said something similar to you? Or have you perhaps said this to yourself? It's a commonly-expressed idea. If you don't relinquish your ties to the one who died, this reasoning goes, then you can't make room for new relationships, new joys, new opportunities in your life. And if you do hang on to that relationship, this same reasoning says, then you're fighting the reality of death and blocking your own grieving process.

What might one say in the face of such advice? Try this: "Not so fast."

This emphasis on severing one's bonds with the deceased is a comparatively recent phenomenon—say, the last hundred years or so—and it's limited to a few industrialized Western cultures. Otherwise, most wisdom through the ages offers the opposite advice: "It's good to find and keep ties with the one you love, even after they have died." It's a message you deserve to hear today.

When someone you love dies, your relationship with that person changes. Some things must come to an end. You cannot do together what you once did. You cannot speak and listen to one another in the same way. You can no longer share physical space and time. That does not mean, however, that you no longer have a relationship at all, or that all communication must be cut off forever. For most survivors, something remains—a link, a bond, a closeness with this one who has been so important.

It is common for a child whose parent has died to find ways to internalize the image of that person who was so instrumental in their formation. It's also common for that internalized image to change as the child matures. Similarly, it's not at all unusual for young and old alike to find comfort in speaking to the one who died, either audibly or inaudibly. Some people report feeling a sense of that person's presence at times, in ways that are hard to describe. Others have a strong impression of seeing or hearing something at one time or another, and they sense this somehow relates to the one they love. The experience usually gives them a kind of peace. More people than you might realize say that they have received strength or assurance or some subtle confirmation that helped them through a difficult time or on a particularly significant day.

How does one explain this? Who knows? Maybe explanations shouldn't be attempted. In an age like today when scientists are continuing to make mind-boggling discoveries about the nature of space and of time, maybe it's enough to say, "Just because something defies easy comprehension doesn't make it any less true."

The great Persian poet Rumi once wrote about his best friend who had died, addressing him with these words: "Now that you live here in my chest, anywhere we sit is a mountaintop." Perhaps his words will ring true for you too, and for the one you love. You can still have a relationship with the one who has died, for they can still live there in your chest, never to leave you, no matter how many other people may come and go through your life. So in addition to letting go in the ways you need to, remember also to hang on in the ways about which you feel right.

10
Your time of loss can be a time of soul-making unlike any other.

The poet John Keats coined the term "soul-making" in a letter written in 1819. Twenty-three years old, he had just nursed his brother to a death by tuberculosis. He had recently learned that he himself would soon die in the same way. He wrote, "Call the world if you please 'the vale of soul-making.' Then you will find out the use of the world."

When you have been confronted with some of life's harsher realities, including the death of someone you love, you too may know the world as a vale, a low point. When that happens, you may discover what Keats and many others have discovered. Merely reflecting on your situation with your mind is not enough. Nor is it enough to simply feel whatever emotions come your way. It's not enough to take care of yourself physically or to find the companionship you need socially. Some other part of you is waiting to be taken into account. That part is your soul.

Everyone has a soul, or perhaps better, everyone is a soul, whether we talk about it much or not. Everyone is a spiritual person, although that spirituality may express itself in many different ways. Some of those ways may appear religious in the traditional sense—participating in worship, for instance, or praying, or reading scriptures. However, you can express yourself spiritually in other ways too—by making time for silence and contemplation, perhaps by immersing yourself in nature, perhaps by using any of the art forms that feel right for you.

The nature of your loss and the experiences of your changing life may naturally lead you to find new ways of expressing yourself spiritually. As much as anything, your journey through grief often entails a search at the deepest level for the meaning of what has happened and what continues to happen. If that is not a spiritual quest, then what is? Your journey can easily put you in touch with the divine dimension—the divine within you and the divine around you. If that is not a spiritual experience, then what is?

You may find that you'll want to focus a little more than usual on the spiritual part of your life. Some people set aside time each day to meditate or pray or just be in solitude. Others take the time to ponder the spiritual aspects of their lives—their faith, their doubts, their significant experiences. There are those who like to meet with a clergyperson or a trained spiritual director on a regular basis. Some others prefer to seek out a spiritual friend—someone who's not necessarily specially trained in spiritual matters but with whom one feels a kinship of the soul. There are also classes, workshops, and retreats you can attend.

While you may yearn for more experiences like this as you grieve, you may be hesitant to engage in these practices too. It takes energy to do this. Moreover, there's much that's unknown, even unknowable, about how all this works. Still, you may hunger deeply for what this experience can offer—a sense of solace, a chance to surrender yourself to something larger, an opportunity to attune yourself to matters more eternal than temporal.

Out of her own grief experience, Emily Dickinson once wrote: "A death blow is a life blow to some." This blow you've been given can put you in touch with some of life's ultimate meanings, which can be life-changing. It can be a time of awakening you'll never forget. Your death blow can become a life blow too, especially if you open yourself to the spiritual dimensions of what is happening to you.

11
Not all your questions will have answers, but they're worth asking anyway.

What has happened to you may lead you to ask some big questions—about the usefulness of prayer, for instance, or the fairness of life, or the justice of God. You may wonder why some people suffer and others do not. You may question why some people go on living, even those who are ready to die, when others who have so much to live for have life taken from them. You may struggle to understand how fate can be so cruel, or how others can be so callous, or how you yourself could have once been so unthinking.

You may feel like hurling questions to anyone, to everyone, to the universe:

- "Why did this have to happen?"
- "Why this one I loved? Why us? Why me?"
- "Why, of all places, here? Why, of all times, now?"

If you have been asking these or similar questions, be assured that you do not stand alone. You join a long, established tradition. Consider, for example, the following questions that go back several millennia:

- "How long must I bear pain in my soul?"
- "What is it that I must wait for?"
- "Why is it that God stands so far away?"

Each of these questions, and many more like them, are found in The Psalms, often considered one of the holiest writings of all time. So people of all sorts and all ages, and people from all the ages, have given voice to these kinds of questions in the face of loss and misfortune. Perhaps the time has come for you to add your voice.

It's possible you may not have many questions as you grieve. Some people, for whatever reasons, are more ready to accept what comes their way. But if questions do surface for you, even troubling ones, it will probably help if you find your own ways to speak them. Your questions can be an expression of your unyielding sadness, your undying love, or your unquenchable longing. Your questioning may be your very honest attempt to draw closer to that which is most real in life, knowing that when you're most authentically yourself, you're no longer hiding. That's a sacred stance.

You'll find that your questioning will eventually lead you into the presence of mystery. Even if you are committed to fathoming all you can, you will eventually find there is something unfathomable. Even if you want to know the unknown, you will discover that some things are forever unknowable. That may be one of the lessons of your grief.

The German writer Rainer Rilke, exchanging letters with a young man who said he himself wanted to be a writer one day, offered this advice: "Be patient toward all that is unsolved in your heart and try to love the questions themselves.... And the point is, to live everything. Live the questions now. Perhaps you will then gradually, without noticing it, live along some distant day into the answer."

Whether you can believe it yet or not, that's a real possibility for you. By living with your questions, by letting them be, by being patient with them as they are, you may find they will lead you to some of the answers you're hoping for. But these are not answers you can force. They come to you when the time is right and you are ready. And then they will come with a sureness you'll not forget.

12
Your time of loss can be a time of discovery.

The talented English writer Katherine Mansfield died much too young at the age of 33. In the last year of her life she wrote these words in her journal: "I do not want to die without leaving a record of my belief that suffering can be overcome. For I do believe it. This is a time to lose oneself more utterly, to love more deeply, to feel oneself a part of life—not separate."

What Katherine Mansfield learned is what you can learn, what we all can learn. Your time of loss can be more than just a time of loss, no matter how much you hurt, no matter how much you wish your life were different. This is a time when something can be added to your life as well as taken away. This is a time when you can become more a part of life than separated from it, however contradictory that may seem.

It may be too early for you to entertain this idea with ease. It may make no sense to you that something helpful could come from this experience. You may feel angry that this could even be true, that the world is made in such a way that anything of worth could come from something that hurts you so much. But it is true. And because many others—most others, in fact—who have undergone serious loss have discovered this same truth, then it is worth noting and affirming.

Your experience of loss may lead you in new directions, directions you might not expect. Chances are you'll become stronger as a result of these trials. You'll become better prepared to handle whatever your future may hold. You'll probably become more self-reliant and self-assured as you work your way through your grief. You're likely to become more resilient, more adaptable, perhaps more open.

One thing you can discover as you grieve, therefore, is yourself, or at least some parts of yourself. You have the possibility of knowing yourself in ways you never have. Inevitably, you'll find yourself changing as you go through this experience. But you'll be doing more than just changing—you'll be maturing.

As you let others into your life, if ever so gradually, maybe even ever so reluctantly, you can develop deepening relationships with those you've long known and those who have come later to your life. Because you've seen it happen, you'll be able to know how families can grow through these experiences, how ties can become stronger, how time spent together may become more meaningful.

Your intimate knowledge of living with endings and adapting to losses can influence how you decide to spend your present moments. It can lead you to reassess your priorities and to work toward enhancing the quality of your own life, as well as life around you. It can help you uncover important lessons about what love really is and how it really works, and it may be different than you once thought. You may discover the presence of the Divine in ways that are new to you, ways that are yet ever so old. In time you may begin to see the universe with fresh eyes, and a fresh spirit, and a fresh hope. It's happened to many, many others. It can also happen to you.

A Final Word.

This time of loss is a time you will not forget. It is a time that is breaking you open and re-shaping you. You will not be the same.

Remember: you can shape this time, even as it is shaping you. You are not entirely at the mercy of whatever has happened to you. You are not completely powerless. It may feel that way to you at the moment. You may wonder if you'll ever regain control of your life. The truth is this: you will and you won't, and that's good.

You will regain more control over your life with the passing of time and in the living of your days. Your hurt will decrease. Your feelings of emptiness will subside. You'll be able to look back and see more of the happiness. You'll face the future and begin to feel you have more to look forward to. You'll sense you're becoming more yourself again.

And, at the same time, you *won't* regain control. For you're coming to know that ultimately much of life is beyond your control, and beyond anyone's control. Life can be lived, but it cannot be contained. It can be appreciated, but it cannot be too narrowly confined. It can be embraced, but it cannot be held too tightly. For in the truest sense, life is nothing less than a gift. It comes from far beyond us, and that is also its destiny, just as that's the destiny of all of us.

Both because of what's happened to you, and despite what's happened to you, may you be on the path of living your life for all it's worth. And never forget: your life is worth a great deal, just as is the life of the one you love.

An Affirmation for Those Who Have Lost

I believe there is no denying it: it hurts to lose.
It hurts to lose a cherished relationship with another,
    as well as a significant part of one's own self.
It can hurt to lose that which has anchored you with the past,
    or that which has beckoned you into the future.
It is painful to feel diminished or cut off or abandoned,
    to be left behind or left alone.
Yet I believe there is more to losing than just the hurt and the pain.
For there are other experiences loss can call forth.
I believe that courage often appears, however quietly it's expressed,
    however easily it goes unnoticed by others:
        the courage to be strong enough to surrender,
            the fortitude to be firm enough to be flexible,
                the bravery to go where you have not gone before.
I believe a time of loss can be a time of learning unlike any other,
    and that it can teach some of life's most valuable lessons:
In the act of losing, there is something to be found.
In the act of letting go, there is something to be grasped.
In the act of saying "goodbye," there is a "hello" to be heard.
For I believe living with loss is about beginnings as well as endings.
And grieving is a matter of life more than of death.
And growing is a matter of mind and heart and soul more than of body.
And loving is a matter of eternity more than of time.
I believe in the promising paradoxes of loss:
In the midst of darkness, there can come a great Light.
In the middle of despair, there can appear a great Hope.
And deep within loneliness, there can dwell a great Love.
I believe these things because others have shown the way—
    others who have lost and then have grown through their losing,
        others who have suffered
            and through their suffering found new meaning.
Finally, I believe whoever we are, whatever has happened to us,
    we are not alone.
We are accompanied, day after day.
We are held, night after night.
We are connected, both here and in eternity.

—James E. Miller

An Affirmation of Those Who Care

I believe in people who care.
Even more, I believe in what these generous people offer others.
They bring caregiving down to its essentials:
    they offer not abstract ideas, but personal attention;
        not definitive answers, but reasonable assurance;
            not empty platitudes, but authentic hope.
I believe the work they do
    is both deceptively simple and unusually difficult.
For their task is to offer those who so need it something irreplaceable:
    their own humanness.
They bestow a priceless gift:
    themselves, and the best of themselves.
They approach the other holding out what they have to offer:
    their sensitivity, their belief, their dedication.
They bring into the open what they choose not to hide:
    their woundedness, their honesty, their compassion.
What these empathetic people do requires real courage,
    for they do not know how they will be received,
        or if they will be understood.
What they give requires great perseverance,
    for healing is a time-consuming process,
        and staying with others in their pain
            is an energy-draining experience.
But if these souls did not perform their roles in the way they do,
    then in a very real sense the Word would not be made flesh.
The Love would not be made visible.
And the Hope would not be made genuine.
Yet because such committed caregivers are among us,
    we know the world is not just a better place
        but ours is a better time and we are a better people.
We know that because those who truly care show us,
    day after day after day.

—James E. Miller

How Can I Help?

James E. Miller is a counselor, writer, photographer, and spiritual director who lives and works in Fort Wayne, Indiana. He lectures, leads workshops, and conducts retreats throughout North America, often utilizing his personal photography to illustrate his ideas. He has created many resources, including books, videotapes, and audiotapes, focusing on illness and dying, caregiving, loss and grief, older age, managing transition, spirituality, and hope. He is married to Bernie and together they have three children.

For information about his various resources, many of which can be purchased in quantity at sizable discounts, as well as about scheduling him for a speaking engagement, contact

Willowgreen
10351 Dawson's Creek Boulevard, Suite B
Fort Wayne, Indiana 46825
260/490-2222

jmiller@willowgreen.com

How Can I Help?

*12 Things to Do
When Someone You Know
Suffers A Loss*

James E. Miller

WILLOWGREEN®
PUBLISHING

Someone you know is grieving. Perhaps you know this person well. They may even be a member of your own family. Or perhaps you haven't been all that close to them, but now, for whatever reason, you feel a connection. Their grief is very real to you.

If you're like many, you may wonder how you can best be with this person who's in such pain over their loss. How do you serve as a good companion to them through this period of their life? What are the things you can do to help them? What should you avoid doing? What might you keep in mind when you're with them, and when you're away from them? How do you know if what you're doing is what's best? These are the kinds of questions this book attempts to answer.

You are not alone in your wondering. Many people feel unsure about how to deal with those who are grieving. You may not yet have experienced deep grief in your own life. You may not have been around other grieving people before. You may have come to realize that our culture does not give us much help by way of mourning rituals or by the natural acceptance of death and all that accompanies it. Consequently, you may have many valid reasons to feel hesitant about your role.

I hope this book will help you. It will not answer all your questions, but I hope it will answer enough that you will feel more confident and more comfortable in your role. Whoever is grieving deserves to have someone like you around them, someone like you who can show that you care. I believe you can make a real difference in their life. I hope you will choose to do so.

Jim Miller

1
Acknowledge what has happened.

After a serious loss has shaken the life of someone they know, people sometimes say to themselves, "I don't want to upset them by mentioning what's happened, so I'll just conveniently sidestep it in conversation." Or they decide, "They know how I feel anyway, so I don't need to tell them." Or they think, "I just don't know what to say in circumstances like this, so I'd best not say anything at all."

You may have had thoughts like these yourself. Many people do. Often behind this hesitation to talk about what has happened is a sense of awkwardness or embarrassment. What if I say the wrong thing? What if I bungle my words? What if the other person cries? What if I cry?

Truth is, those who are grieving the death of another usually want to have their situation acknowledged by people they know and respect. It communicates that others recognize the significance of what has happened to them. It validates their tumultuous feelings. It links them with a community of others who care, and it provides visible evidence that support is likely to be there in the future when they need it. Acknowledging this loss serves as a bridge—a bridge from life-as-it-used-to-be to life-as-it-is-becoming. Unless you communicate to the other person that you're aware of what has happened and that you have feelings about it, you cannot proceed to relate with this person at any real depth.

There are many ways to make your acknowledgment, depending on your relationship with the other person and your own level of comfort. You might telephone them, voicing your sympathy and offering your support. You might express what you feel the next time you see that person, assuming you expect to see them soon. You might send a card, or write a short note, or spell out your thoughts in a longer letter. You might choose to deliver a dish or a meal, send a flower or a plant, or perform some other small act of kindness, all as a way of saying, "I realize this death has taken its toll on you and I want you to know you are on my mind."

Sometimes special sensitivity may be called for. In rare circumstances a person or a family may deny their loss has occurred. Or it may simply be that they are not prepared to admit it to others just yet. Some deaths may be more difficult to talk about because of how they occurred. Complicated family dynamics may cloud the situation. And it's worth noting that there are a handful of people who really don't want to have their loss acknowledged—that's just the way they are.

But the vast majority of grieving people appreciate being reminded that others understand the seriousness of what has happened. They may not remember exactly what you said or did in that first encounter with them after their loss, but they will not forget you were there, emotionally if not physically. And they are likely to draw real meaning from what you chose to say and do.

People who are grieving often feel different from others. They can feel cut off, pushed aside, ignored. When you reach out to open the line of communciation, you're saying in effect, "I am with you and I *will* be with you." That can be a very powerful and assuring message.

2
Listen. Listen. Listen.

When an important part of another's life has ended and they did not want it to end, at the very least they experience discomfort or pain, and they may feel much more: shock, numbness, disbelief, anxiety. They may feel anger, if not rage. They may experience deep guilt, or overpowering sadness, or disturbing fear. They may feel as if their life were racing out of control. They may wonder if they're going a little crazy.

People in grief need to make sense of what has occurred in their life. One way they can do that is to talk about what has happened around them and within them. Usually, they need to tell their story, and they need others to hear that story, in order to validate its significance.

A thoughtful gift you can give one who's grieving is the invitation for them to speak what's on their mind and heart. Usually it doesn't take much: "Tell me about what happened. I'd like to know." Your honest concern and curiosity will encourage their words. Don't probe unneccessarily—let them decide what they're ready to reveal. Honor their own sense of timing.

You'll find it's common for people in such circumstances to want to speak longer than normal. They have much to say. They may have many details they want to convey. They may repeat themselves. They may get parts of their story mixed up. They may stop and start their tale more than once, making it difficult to follow their train of thought.

However much they talk, and in whatever way they talk, remember they are doing what they most need to do. They are finding ways to understand and accept what has come crashing into their life. They may feel they're trying to preserve their sanity in what seems an insane time. With each telling and retelling, they begin to grasp a little more of what this death means for their life. By naming what has occurred and by forming words that approximate something of what is going on inside them, they begin their adjustment to the enormity of this new reality.

How can you be a good listener for someone who's grieving? Find a quiet place where you can be together, free of potential disruptions if possible. If you can, sit rather than stand, and sit facing one another. The other person may feel weak or tired and appreciate being off their feet. In addition, your sitting communicates your willingness to stay awhile—you won't bolt away. It also puts you on the same eye level.

Make sure your nonverbal language says what you want it to, including your facial expression, the way you hold your body, the way you maintain your gaze. Remember that if you say something with your mouth and then you say something different with the rest of your body, the other person will believe, not your words, but everything else you're communicating.

Good listening takes energy. It can be both time-consuming and tiring to stay with another in their grief. It can be emotionally draining. And, at the same time, your listening can be an act of sacredness—you create an environment in which someone can entrust you with the essence of who they are, what they think and feel, what they fear and hope.

Over the course of time the two of you can experience something wonderful together—the healing that begins to take place gradually as their story is told and re-told, as they begin to make adjustments in their days, as they start to trust life again. It all begins with this: your willingness to stay with them and simply listen. It is a greater gift than you may realize.

3
Respond in your own authentic way.

Whether the other person talks very little, as is sometimes the case, or at great length, she or he will benefit if you do more than listen—you respond. They will appreciate knowing they've been understood by what you say. They will feel validated that what they're experiencing and what they're doing are reasonable for these unusual circumstances.

You may wonder about the best way to respond. As long as what you say is genuine for you, and as long as you have the other's best interests at heart, chances are you will be helpful. It's not important that your words be polished. It's important that they be honest and real. Sometimes it's impossible to improve upon words like these: "I don't know what to say at the moment. I don't have words. But I do care."

Several kinds of responses will help communication flow. Letting people know what you feel usually frees both them and you to talk more freely and perhaps on a deeper level. When you summarize what the other person has said and reflect it back to them, it helps both of you understand one another better. Try asking questions if you're unsure what the other person has meant. Put any feelings they express in your own words and see how close you can come to identifying what's going on inside them. Show them that you're prepared to accept whatever they have to say. As you converse, use the name of the person who died. This helps recall that person's presence and it confirms they have not been forgotten and will not be.

Avoid using clichés—those commonly used expressions that are intended to help the other feel better but in actuality often have the opposite effect. Examples are:

• *"I know exactly how you feel."* No you don't, because you're not that other person and you haven't experienced their same loss. In using those words, you tend to discount the uniqueness of their feelings.

• *"You must be as strong as you can be now."* In our culture "being strong" is often made synonymous with holding in one's emotions. During a time of loss, chances are that's not necessarily the best way to deal with one's grief. Finding one's own ways to give voice to what's going on inside is a part of a grieving person's healing process.

• *"You should count your blessings."* Any response that contains the word "should" is likely to be received as heavy-handed. Moreover, too much emphasis on blessings early in one's adjustment may deny the grief that needs to be experienced.

• *"It was God's will"* and *"God never gives you more than you can handle"* may be your personal belief, but it may not ring true for the other, especially if he or she is angry that God has allowed something so devastating to happen.

Be slow to offer advice unless you're asked for it. Even if you believe you know what's best, the other may not be ready to hear. And what's best for you may not be best for them.

Remember there are ways other than using words to respond to someone who's grieving. Thoughtful silence can sometimes convey closeness in a way sound cannot. A touch or a hug may be terribly expressive. And sometimes it is your tears, mingled with theirs, that speak volumes and remove any doubt as to whether or not you are really with them.

4
Accept the other as he or she is.

As people grieve, they may not act like their normal selves. They may cry unexpectedly or uncontrollably. Or they may not weep at all. They may talk an unusual amount, which means they may be especially wordy or especially quiet. They may be very expressive with their emotions, or they may appear more impassive. They may want to be around others a lot, or they may prefer to spend much of their time alone. They may turn naturally to those who have been close friends, and then again they may pull away from these same people.

You will help the one you care about if you can suspend judgment about how they are responding, especially in the early part of their grief. Understand they are doing the best they can, given who they are and what has happened to them. They may be in shock for awhile. Their behavior may seem erratic. They may have difficulty making decisions. They may change their mind a lot. They may cling more than usual. They may get mad without warning. During this trying time of their life, what they need above all is understanding and acceptance.

It's not uncommon for a person in grief to feel as if they're separated from those around them. In a sense they are, for no one else is going through exactly what they're going through, even if they're members of the same family, even if they've experienced the same loss. People in grief may feel odd and out of place, as if they don't belong anywhere. They may feel as if they're shunned by others. Their self-esteem may drop. They may question their ability to cope.

By accepting a person like this as they are at the moment, you encourage them to continue doing what they feel they need to do as they make their way through their grief. For some, that is to feel the full strength of their emotions, so they can move *through* those feelings rather than *around* them. Others may choose to delay those feelings for awhile, until they are more ready to deal with all that has happened and to face what this means for their future.

Accept that they know their own needs better than you. And they will be working with their own timetable for their grief. It is unfair and even unhealthy to impose your own schedule on them, especially if you have not known a loss like theirs. Even if you have, your ways of working through times of difficult transition will not work for everyone. You're too different and so are your situations.

By reaching out to the other with warmth and compassion, and by respecting their right to learn for themselves as they live their way through this jolting experience, you offer them a kind of positive regard that will help strengthen them for their tasks ahead.

There's something else to remember: the most effective way to accept another is to accept yourself first. So if you really want to support other people during difficult times in their lives, you will do well to be conscious of how accepting you are of your own emotions, your own fluctuations, your own foibles, and your own shortcomings. The better friend you can be to yourself, the better friend you'll make for others.

5
Offer to help, and make your offers specific.

"Let me know if there's anything at all I can do to help."
How many times have you heard someone say that? Have you
ever said it yourself? However sincere it may sound, more often
than not this is an offer that goes nowhere. People who are
reeling with the pain of their loss may not have the energy or
inclination to follow up with this kind of overture. They may
feel uncomfortable or embarrassed in needing assistance. They
may doubt that your offer is sincere, because some offers like
that are not.

If you want to help a person who's grieving, be clear about
what you say and how you say it. Ask them specifically about
what you can do. Give them some options. Allow them time to
respond. Be understanding if they change their mind.

Don't act as if you know exactly what they need. You don't.
Make sure they maintain some sense of control by giving them
the option to say "no" with a certain ease. If they do say "no,"
treat this as a friendly refusal for that particular offer. Make
other offers later. Keep letting them know you're serious about
being available, but always treat their answer with respect.
Don't push.

Following are examples of what you might say by way of
wanting to help:

• "I'd like to bring in a meal for you and your family. I'll be
cooking a big meal already next Tuesday and Thursday.
Would either day work for you?"

• "We've had a lot of experience getting houses ready for
winter. We'd like to lend a hand with yours if you're interested.
How about one Saturday next month?"

• "I can't imagine how you maintain your caregiving re-
sponsibilities without some time away. Would it be helpful if I

were to spend an afternoon or an evening in your home so you can get away for awhile? Are there certain times you need to be gone?"

Offers of your time are among the most thoughtful gifts you can make. This includes personal visits, invitations to dinner or an evening out, and "just-checking-in" telephone calls. You might volunteer to be a part of that person's "buddy system," ready to receive their telephone calls anytime of the day or night, should that be needed. You might also stay in touch by email, which allows more flexibility in when they hear from you and how they respond, or with cards and notes, which they can keep and read more than once if they want. You might consider the loan or the gift of an article or book, an audiotape or videotape. But don't give something without having read it or experienced it first, at least in part, so that you're sure of its quality and its appropriateness.

Among the best offers are those that are uniquely yours. Do what you're good at, what feels natural, what you enjoy. Very important is this: do what you say you're going to do, when you say you're going to do it. It's likely the person you're relating to will be feeling that the world is not as secure a place as it once was. They're looking for all the dependability they can find.

Don't forget that it's usually easier to provide help early on when the need may be more obvious. But some of the most valuable help you can provide may come months and even years later, when most of the others have turned their attention away from the loss and yet that person's healing is still in process.

6
Allow the other her or his privacy.

This suggestion to give the other their space may seem to contradict the previous ideas about being present and listening and responding. But that is not so. Encouraging others to have their own privacy is simply an additional way of being with them and of letting them know you care.

Grieving people often discover their time alone becomes very important to them. They may need their solitary time more, and they may need *more* such time, than during other periods of their lives.

As they grieve, people tend to feel vulnerable and exposed. They may feel as if a lot of people are watching them (and they probably are). Their pockets of privacy can become those times when they begin to create an oasis of safety and security around them. They may also experience a pervading sense of loneliness, and they may feel that most strongly, not when they're alone, but when they're in the presence of others.

Private moments allow people to do the vital introspective work that is theirs and no one else's to do. They need to process what has happened, and to consider what may yet happen. They often need to think and to meditate, to ponder and to mourn, to remember and to plan. They may relish their time just to read, to write, or to work with their hands. They may wish to claim their right to do nothing at all. And often, of course, when one does nothing, one is doing a great deal. Don't forget too that the other person may simply enjoy their own company and the peacefulness of their own quiet.

You can be a steadying influence in several ways. You can counterbalance those messages that others may be sending— messages like "you must keep yourself busy" or "too much time alone is not good for you." You can honor the other's call for solitude. You can protect them from the thoughtless intrusion of others, and that can include the intrusion of yourself.

One reason caring individuals sometimes have difficulty allowing grieving people their privacy relates to the difficulty they experience in their role as caregivers. There is a helplessness that goes with being a helper. No matter how much one wants to do or is able to do for another, there is still much that cannot be done. The other's pain cannot be taken away. The other's healing cannot be hurried. The other's learning experiences cannot be circumvented. Everyone must live with this reality.

Everyone must live as well with the reality that people who are able to grow from their losses must take responsibility for their own lives. If others do too much for them over the long haul, if others make too many decisions in their place, then everyone's lives are the poorer.

A final word about privacy: sometimes there can be too much of it. If over the course of a number of months the other person becomes unusally reclusive, seldom venturing out and seldom allowing others in, then more direct action may be in order. This might entail your encouraging them to get out more, and maybe even helping make that happen. You might meet with family members to listen to their feedback and enlist their support. You might choose simply to invite them to lunch more regularly, or to invite them into your home more often.

In general, though, respect the privacy of the other as they grieve. It's more than their right—it can be their lifeblood.

7
Relate to the other as a whole person.

Grief makes itself known through all parts of a person. It expresses itself through their whole being—body, mind, heart, and soul. Each aspect of who they are is an avenue for the healing of their grief. The root word for "heal" is the same as the root word for "whole." To heal as you grieve means to open to your whole self as you grieve.

You can help the one you're companioning by paying attention with them to the physical aspects of their grief responses. You can normalize the various ways grief expresses itself through the body. Tightness across the chest and in the throat, hollowness in the stomach, pain around one's heart, headaches, nausea, diarrhea, and other physical responses are quite common. You can underline the absolute importance of taking care of their physical selves as they grieve by eating well, getting the rest they need, and exercising. You can support them in caring for themselves by seeing a physician for a physical exam, perhaps by getting massages, or by pampering themselves in those ways that make them feel and look better.

Relating to them as a physical person may include touching them or holding them, depending on who they are and your relationship with them. Some grieving people feel touch-deprived, especially if the one who died was their major source of physical intimacy. Still, some individuals prefer not to be touched. They find it uncomfortable, even invasive. A good rule of thumb is to touch gently and appropriately, and to make it easy and natural for the other person to move away if that's what they prefer.

Much of what's considered caregiving for someone who's grieving involves relating to their heart or their emotional self. Many such ideas appear elsewhere throughout these pages.

Essentially this includes listening to their feelings, encouraging and validating their feelings however they express them, as well as reflecting and responding to their feelings.

Making room for one's mind, one's mental capacity, as a griever may mean helping them seek information about the process of grief in general or their own grief response in particular. Whether it's by talking, reading, or undertaking some form of study, you can support them in their efforts to understand intellectually what's happening to them. You can also normalize the way grief expresses itself through their mental processes—in being absent-minded, for instance, or in finding it hard to concentrate, or in needing to learn in small, short doses.

Usually grief affects them spiritually as well. It may show itself in any religious observances of theirs (more of them or fewer of them), in how or whether they pray or meditate, with their questions about the meaning of what has happened. For many grieving people, this is a time when their sense of spirituality is awakened and perhaps challenged. As you spend time with someone who's grieving, remember that their grief will flow out through all parts of who they are. Remember also that all these parts of themselves can be avenues by which their grief can be approached, a little at a time. You can help them understand that. Mostly, you can relate to them through all parts of who you are. Your wholeness encourages their wholeness.

8
Trust the other to lead you.

However good you are as a caregiver, however many others you've companioned through grief, this fact remains: you are not the person who's in charge here. This is not your loss, nor is it your grief. It is theirs. They know more about what is happening to them than you do. So you will do well to listen to them and learn from them.

It's clear that every person's journey through grief is absolutely unique. It's equally clear that grief is a natural, normal process that enables a person to heal from their loss. While grief is commonly associated with the death of someone close, it also follows many other sorts of losses: separation and divorce, the ending of one's job, the loss of one's health or one's home or one's future. Grief will result even from the loss of intangible things, like the loss of innocence, or security, or hope. When any loss occurs, a built-in human mechanism is set to go to work to help this person respond to what has happened. This self-limiting, self-directing grief has its own wisdom. It knows what it needs, if it's allowed its options. It knows what to do, if it's given room to do it. It will work its magic, if it's given time. In short, grief will usually lead the one you're companioning, who can in turn lead you.

This may be a different kind of leading than you're used to. The path beneath your feet may not be as direct as you expect or desire. As you walk with this other person, it may even seem like you're going in circles sometimes, or like you're lost other times. You may be led to places you'd rather not go—places of darkness, or coldness, or bleakness. But it will help the other person if you continue to follow their lead, accepting the ups and downs of this journey, staying with them even in the midst of the unknown.

What will happen as you do this? The other person will teach you about how this experience has changed their life, and continues to change it. They will instruct you about what encourages their healing and what doesn't, what helps their pain and what hurts them even more. They will be able to inform you, if you let them, about how they maintain their connection with the one they love, and maybe even communciate with them, as mysterious as that may seem.

If you stay open with one another, they can let you know how well you're companioning them, and what might help them a little more. That will improve this experience both for them and for you. It will also improve similar experiences you'll have with others some day. And it can prepare you, at least a little, for your own experiences of loss that await you, just as they await everyone.

The more you trust their process of grief, the more they will trust it too. The more you trust them, the more they can trust themselves and the more they will come to trust you. In allowing yourself to be led, you will be taught how to provide the kind of leadership they need.

9
Radiate genuine hope.

When someone has been devastated by a deep sense of loss, they may feel their happiness has ended, never to return. Depression and despair may settle in, making the world look gray and bleak. The future may be very short on hope.

Your more objective perspective is different. You can understand their melancholy, but you also know that melancholy does not need to have the last word. Problems that seem insurmountable can usually be surmounted, one way or another. Shocks can be absorbed. Losses can be assimilated with time. Lives can be renewed. But those possibilities may not be obvious to the one in your care. She or he may not wish to believe those possibilities could even exist at all.

Yours is a tender task. You understand their sorrow and you're prepared to wait with them in that dark place. Yet you also believe that one day the light *will* return. You know that authentic hope can be a literal lifesaver, yet you also know that unrealistic promises can be more than disappointing—they can be destructive. People need assurance things will get better, yet the timing of that assurance is critical—not too much too early, and not too little too late.

What can you do as a person who genuinely cares? You can radiate hope that is both appropriate for the other and true for you. In your unique way you can present what your experience teaches you is real and what your conviction tells you is possible. Words are an obvious way to do that. This can be as simple as stating what you believe: "I believe you will one day feel better." Or, "You *will* see the light of day again. It's happened to every person I've known who has gone through this sort of thing." When the time seems right, you can tell them about other people who have loved and lost and learned to love again. You can remind these people how they have persevered in the past. You can give them feedback about the specific ways you see them making progress today.

You can provide encouragement with cards and other written messages. It's affirming to have something you can physically hold and look at, something to which you can return when you wish. Inspirational books and tapes are popular for just that reason.

Try adding your own personal touch to what you want to share. Locate articles that apply to that person's situation and pass them on, along with your own reflections. Share with them something you've written yourself. Be on the lookout for talks or motivational messages that have just the right tenor. Pass along an uplifting song or album or movie. Create an original cassette tape of music from various artists, or some meaningful readings, or a combination of the two. Record your own voice saying what you most want them to hear and to remember. For those who are more visually oriented, a picture or a poster or a video may communicate its own positive message for months and years to come.

Probably the most effective vehicle for conveying hope is simply this one: you. Your attitude toward life and love is always on display. Hope is not something you merely talk about, something you promise. It's something you live, something you embody.

Should the other person find it difficult to hope, you might do this: let them know that you will hold their hope for them until they're ready to hold it again on their own. Then do what you say—hold their hope for them day by day, consciously, willingly, lovingly.

10
Carry the other in your heart and soul.

It's not important to make sure the other person knows all about your caring actions on their behalf. Quiet and private acts can be just as effective as visible and public ones—maybe more so.

If you're truly linked with another person, they're with you when you're apart as well as when you're together. You remember them in various ways throughout your days and nights. You make your remembrance of them intentional.

Depending upon your personal practices, you might make them a part of your regular prayer or meditation. You might include them in some way in any experience of corporate worship, or perhaps in prayer chains or prayer groups. You might adopt an age-old practice known as "kything" in which you simply bring the other person into your consciousness and hold them there for a little while each day. Kything is not so much praying as it is "well-wishing" or "love-sending." You can bring the other with you as you perform a small ritual while thinking of them—lighting a candle, for instance, or holding an object that reminds you of them, or carrying something on your person that links you with them.

You might include that person in your journal writing by penning your hopes and dreams for them. If you're artistic, you might create some work of art with their spirit in mind. Whether you give it to them or keep it for yourself, the art can continue doing its own good.

Some intriguing research is taking place about what happens to people in their healing when they are prayed for or intentionally remembered by others. There is evidence that this can make an identifiable difference. But even without that research, personal experience can tell you the same thing.

Carrying another does not necessarily mean forming specific words or praying for concrete results. Maybe you're not even sure what's best for them at the moment, or what they need. Bringing their face or their person to mind and holding it there in silent wordlessness can work its own kind of power. It's possible to carry the other even *un*intentionally, as you dream at night, for example, or as you pay attention to your intuition.

Should you adopt any of these practices, keep in mind the value of remembering the other person regularly, consistently. Be aware prayers of celebration or writings of gratitude are as important as thoughts of concern. Of course, it makes sense to remember this person in special ways during those times you know to be particularly important for them—during periods of testing or times of doubt, on anniversaries of special events, or during emotion-laden seasons of the year.

You may choose to tell the other person that you're making a place for them in your quiet moments. Most people find that an affirming thought and are pleased to know they linger with another in that way. But it probably doesn't matter whether you talk about what you're doing or not. Somehow the one you care about will know.

11
Journey with the other in the search for meaning.

Companioning another on their walk through grief involves more than giving them the opportunity to express their sorrow, anger, and depression. It involves more than doing chores that help them and providing the kind of support that boosts them. Real companionship involves taking a larger look at what has happened and continues to happen. It involves looking for those lessons that have been learned, can be learned, and are in process of being learned. Really being with another includes watching for any blessings that may appear, however small, and highlighting any experiences of grace that may occur, however subtle. It involves being open to all the meaning that can be found.

This is no easy task. Sometimes there are no sure answers. Sometimes the meaning may change, either as people grow or as events unfold. Sometimes there may appear to be no meaning at all to what has happened, and to search for some underlying significance may trivialize the gravity or the horror of this loss.

Still, this caring journey with another is not complete until you each stand back, as if from a distance, and consider certain questions that might help illuminate or bring clarity to these events. These various queries are seldom stated as simply as they appear here, but you might talk over together some of following issues:

• What are you discovering about yourself as you go through this experience? Your strengths? Your new growing edges? What's becoming of the person you used to be?

• What has happened to you when you've had to surrender your will? Has surrender had any value for you? Has it given you anything?

- What have you learned about relationships, yours with others and theirs with you? The energy of relationships? The power? The importance?
- What perspective do you have about the way your life used to be compared to the way it is today? Is there anything to learn about what's important and what's not? About where you find happiness, and how? About how love works?
- Do you see the world around you any differently as a result of what you've been through? If so, how?
- What doubts are you having to face, and where are they leading you? What do you now believe more deeply than ever? Have you come to know anything about a divine presence working its way through these days? What has that experience taught you?
- What have you learned about the nature of death? About what death can do and what it cannot do? About what death teaches you about life?
- What do you believe about your place in the world? About what your future holds for you? About what you now have to offer?

Journeys through loss hold the potential for becoming journeys of deep meaning, meaning that will not be forgotten. While these quests must at times be solitary ones, there are other times when the presence of a person who cares will make the difference between someone continuing on that journey and stopping in one's tracks. When someone like you journeys alongside, you provide not just company—you help create possibility.

12
Open yourself to what this experience holds just for you.

When you companion another through grief, something happens to you as well as to that other person. It is unavoidable.

If you've known the one who died, chances are you'll be feeling something of what the other one is, even if it's less intensely. Even if you have not known the one who died, your companion's loss may touch you at a deep level. English psychiatrist Colin Parkes once wrote about the situation of which you're a part: "Pain is inevitable and cannot be avoided. It stems from the awareness of both parties that neither can give the other what they want. The helper cannot bring back the person who is dead, and the bereaved cannot gratify the helper by seeming helped." In other words, you'll have your own discomfort just from trying to comfort another.

There's another level of unease you may feel, summed up in the poetic words of John Donne: "Never send to know for whom the (funeral) bell tolls. It tolls for thee." As you companion another, you're constantly reminded that death may claim someone you love too, and that grief will visit you, just as it's visiting them. But that's not all. Death may take, not just someone you love, but you! And not just "*may* take" but "*will* take"! You stand face-to-face with death's uncompromising realities when you stand side-by-side with someone who's grieving the loss of one they have loved.

But there is more to what this experience can hold for you. There are hidden benefits to this work that you do as a caregiver. Anyone who is confronted with the limits death places on life is also confronted with something more: the preciousness that death adds to life. Once you realize in a first-hand way how fleeting life is, you can no longer take it for granted. Once you appreciate how extraordinary this life is—and not just this life but these people, this earth, this universe—then you look at all that is around you with different eyes. You walk with a different step.

Just as the one you companion is changed by the journey they must take, so you are changed by this journey that you take *with* them. Because of all that you see and hear, you become more aware, more mature, more knowing. Because of all you're led to say and do, you become more flexible, more understanding, more compassionate. It's likely that out of these experiences that stretch you, you learn how to be a better caregiver, and you can carry that knowledge with you into the future. It's likely you'll become not just wiser but gentler, not just more forgiving but more loving. Ultimately you'll become not just a better listener but a better friend, not just a better caregiver but a better human being. And that's not a bad trade-off.

A Final Word.

Assisting another through their loss is not a task to be taken lightly. It takes time, perhaps more than you expect. It requires patience, perhaps more than you're ready for. It calls for your perseverance, your flexibility, your optimism. Most of all, it asks of you your understanding, your warmth, and your compassion.

After reading these suggestions for what you can do for another, you may wonder if you have it in you to be a good caregiver. That's not uncommon. It's one reason why grieving people may find it such a lonely experience—available caregivers may be standing back, wondering what they have to give.

If this is your reaction, try saying this to yourself: "I am enough." If you really want to help another, and if your heart is in the right place, then it's true: you *are* enough. Whatever your professional skills and whatever your experiences, you are enough. Whatever your personal strengths and whatever your limits, you are enough.

You see, if you had only strengths and no limits, if you possessed all the skills available and made no mistakes, then you would be *not* enough. The person who is struggling and grieving needs someone beside them who can understand, someone who can identify with them, someone as human as they are. They need someone like you.

It comes down to this:

If not now, then when?

If not here, then where?

If not you, then who?